RUBANK EDUCATIONAL LIBRARY No. 175

RUBANK Advanced Method

FLUTE

Vol. II

H. VOXMAN

AN OUTLINED COURSE OF STUDY
DESIGNED TO FOLLOW UP ANY
OF THE VARIOUS ELEMENTARY
AND INTERMEDIATE METHODS

RUBANK®

HAL•LEONARD®
CORPORATION

7777 W. BLUEMOUND RD. P.O. BOX 13819 MILWAUKEE, WI 53213

NOTE

THE RUBANK ADVANCED METHOD for Flute is published in two volumes, the course of study being divided in the following manner:

Vol. I
{ Keys of C, F, G, Bb, and D Major.
{ Keys of A, D, E, G, and B Minor.

Vol. II
{ Keys of Eb, A, Ab, E, Db, and B Major.
{ Keys of C, F#, F, and C# Minor.

PREFACE

THIS METHOD is designed to follow any of the various Elementary and Intermediate instruction series, or Elementary instruction series comprising two or more volumes, depending upon the previous background of the student. The author has found it necessary in his teaching experience to draw from many sources in order to provide a progressive course of study. The present publication assembles in two volumes, the material essential to a well-rounded musical development.

THE OUTLINES, one of which is included in each of the respective volumes, tend to afford an objective picture of the student's progress. They will facilitate the ranking of members in a large ensemble or they may serve as a basis for awards of merit. In addition, a one-sided development along strictly technical or strictly melodic lines is avoided. The use of these outlines, however, is not imperative and they may be discarded at the discretion of the teacher.

H. Voxman

OUTLINE
OF
RUBANK ADVANCED METHOD
FOR
FLUTE, Vol. II
by H. Voxman

UNIT	SCALES and ARPEGGIOS (Key)					MELODIC INTERPRE-TATION		ARTICU-LATION		FINGER EXERCISES		ORNA-MENTS			SOLOS		UNIT COM-PLETED
1	5	(1)	6	(5)	E♭	20	(1)	50	(1)	61	(1)	64	(1)		74	(1)	
2	5	(2)	6	(6)	E♭	21	(2)	50	(2)	61	(2)	64	(2)		74	(1)	
3	5	(3)	6	(7)	E♭	22	(3)	50	(3)	61	(3)	64	(3)		74	(1)	
4	6	(4)	8		E♭	22	(3)	51	(4)	61	(4)	64	(4)		74	(1)	
5	7	(9)	10		c	24	(4)	51	(5)	61	(5)	65	(5)	(6)	74	(1)	
6	7	(11)	12		c	24	(5)	51	(6)	61	(6)	65	(7)		74	(1)	
7	7	(13)	14		c	26	(6)	51	(6)	61	(7)	66	(8)		76	(2)	
8	8	(15)	9	(19)	A	26	(7)	52	(7)	61	(8)	66	(9)		76	(2)	
9	8	(16)	9	(20)	A	28	(8)	52	(8)	61	(9)	66	(10)		76	(2)	
10	8	(17)	9	(21)	A	28	(8)	52	(9)	61	(10)	67	(11)	(12)	76	(2)	
11	9	(18)	22		A	30	(9)	53	(10)	61	(11) (12)		67	(13)		76	(2)	
12	10	(23)	24		f♯	31	(10)	53	(11)	61	(13)	67	(14)		76	(2)	
13	10	(25)	26		f♯	32	(11)	54	(12)	61	(14)	68	(15)	(16)	77	(3)	
14	10	(27)	28		f♯	32	(12)	54	(13)	61	(15)	68	(17)		77	(3)	
15	11	(29)	12	(33)	A♭	34	(13)	54	(14)	61	(16)	68	(18)		77	(3)	
16	11	(30)	12	(34)	A♭	34	(14)	54	(14)	61	(17)	68	(19)		77	(3)	
17	11	(31)	12	(35)	A♭	35	(15)	55	(15)	61	(18)	69	(20)		77	(3)	
18	11	(32)	12	(36)	A♭	35	(15)	55	(16)	61	(19)	69	(21)	(22)	77	(3)	
19	12	(37)	38		f	36	(16)	55	(17)	61	(20)	69	(22)		78	(4)	
20	13	(39)	40		f	37	(17)	56	(18)	61	(21)	70	(23)		78	(4)	
21	13	(41)	42		f	37	(17)	56	(19)	61	(22)	70	(24)		78	(4)	
22	13	(43)	44		E	38	(18)	56	(20)	61	(23)	70	(25)		78	(4)	
23	14	(45)	47		E	39	(19)	56	(20)	61	(24)	70	(25)		78	(4)	
24	14	(46)			E	40	(20)	57	(21)	61	(25)	71	(26)		78	(4)	
25	14	(48)	49		E	40	(20)	57	(21)	61	(26)	71	(27)		79	(5)	
26	15	(50)	51		c♯	41	(21)	57	(22)	61	(27)	71	(27)		79	(5)	
27	15	(52)	53		c♯	42	(22)	58	(23)	61	(28)	72	(28)		79	(5)	
28	16	(54)	55		c♯	42	(22)	58	(24)	61	(29)	72	(28)		79	(5)	
29	16	(56)			D♭	43	(23)	58	(25)	61	(30)	72	(29)		79	(5)	
30	16	(57)	17	(60)	D♭	44	(24)	58	(26)	61	(31)	72	(29)		79	(5)	
31	16	(58)	17	(61)	D♭	46	(25)	59	(27)	61	(32)	73	(30)		80	(6)	
32	17	(59)	62		D♭	46	(25)	59	(28)	61	(33)	73	(31)		80	(6)	
33	17	(63)	19	(67)	B	47	(26)	59	(29)	61	(34)	73	(32)		80	(6)	
34	18	(64)	19	(68)	B	48	(27)	59	(29)	61	(35)	73	(33)		80	(6)	
35	18	(65)	19	(69)	B	49	(28)	60	(30)	61	(36)	73	(34)		80	(6)	
36	19	(66)	(70)		B	49	(28)	60	(30)	61	(37)	73	(35)		80	(6)	

NUMERALS designate page number.

ENCIRCLED NUMERALS designate exercise number.

COMPLETED EXERCISES may be indicated by crossing out the rings, thus, ⊗.

PRACTICE AND GRADE REPORT

SECOND SEMESTER

Student's Name _____

Date _____

Week	Sun.	Mon.	Tue.	Wed.	Thu.	Fri.	Sat.	Total	Parent's Signature	Grade
1										
2										
3										
4										
5										
6										
7										
8										
9										
10										
11										
12										
13										
14										
15										
16										
17										
18										
19										
20										

Semester Grade _____

Instructor's Signature _____

FIRST SEMESTER

Student's Name _____

Date _____

Week	Sun.	Mon.	Tue.	Wed.	Thu.	Fri.	Sat.	Total	Parent's Signature	Grade
1										
2										
3										
4										
5										
6										
7										
8										
9										
10										
11										
12										
13										
14										
15										
16										
17										
18										
19										
20										

Semester Grade _____

Instructor's Signature _____

Scales and Arpeggios
Eb Major

4

Various articulations may be used in the chromatic, the interval, and the arpeggio exercises at the option of the instructor.

Chromatic Scale

5

Scale in Thirds

6

Common Chord

7

Dominant 7th Chord

8

C Minor

A Major

F# Minor

Natural **Harmonic**

23

Melodic

24

simile

25

simile

simile

Scale in Thirds

26

Common Chord

27

Diminished 7th Chord

28

12

Chromatic Scale

33

Scale in Thirds

34

Common Chord

35

Dominant 7th Chord

36

F Minor

Natural   **Harmonic**

37

Melodic

Practice slurred and tongued.

38

simile

simile

39

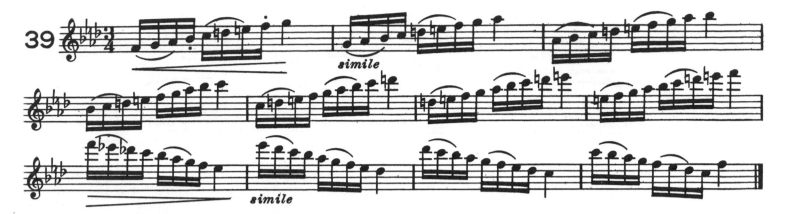

Scale in Thirds

40

Common Chord

41

Diminished 7th Chord

42

E Major

43

44

C# Minor

Common Chord

54

Diminished 7th Chord

55

Db Major

56

57

58

59

Scale in Thirds

60

Common Chord

61

Dominant 7th Chord

62

B Major

63

64

simile

simile

65

simile

66

simile

Chromatic Scale

67

Scale in Thirds

68

Common Chord

69

Dominant 7th Chord

70

Studies in Melodic Interpretation
For One or Two Part Playing

The following studies have been selected with the idea of ensemble performance in mind. Much effort has been expended in selecting duets in which the first and second parts are melodically and rhythmically independent. Students should be encouraged to practice these numbers as duets outside the lesson period. When circumstances permit, any number of students can perform them as an ensemble. The lower part of the duets may be assigned at the discretion of the teacher.

Careful attention to the marks of expression is essential to effective use of the material. Where different dynamic signs are written for the upper and lower parts, observe them accurately. The part having the melody must always slightly predominate even when the dynamic indications are the same.

Pencil the technically difficult passages and devote extra time to their mastery.

In rhythmic music in the more rapid tempi (marches, dances, etc.), tones that are equal divisions of the beat are played somewhat detached (staccato). Tones that equal a beat or are multiples of a beat are held full value. Tones followed by rests are usually held full value. This point should be especially observed in slow music.

The trills in eighteenth century music should generally <u>begin</u> with the note <u>above</u> the main note. This is true in the music of Handel, Haydn, Geminiani, Stamitz, Boismortier, and others.

Air

HANDEL

Lento [*quasi moderato*]

GARIBOLDI

2

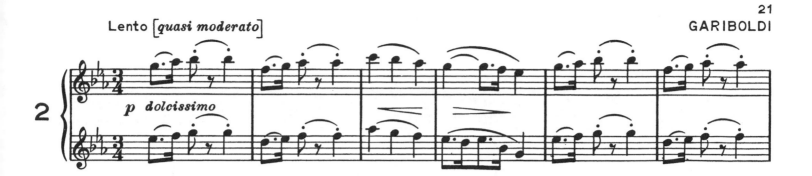

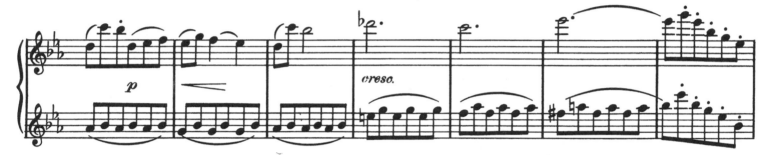

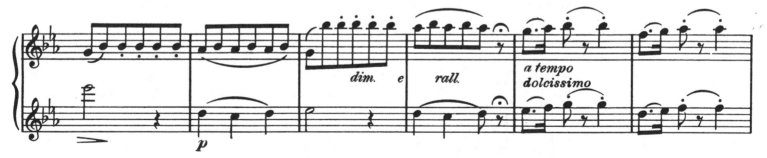

Menuett

HAYDN-BARGE

Fine

TRIO

Menuett D.C.

BOUSQUET

4

H. KÖHLER

5

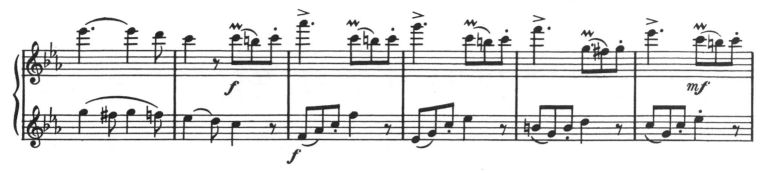

Adagio [non troppo]

GEMINIANI

6

Romance

Andante [in moderate four]

STAMITZ

7

Allegretto

8

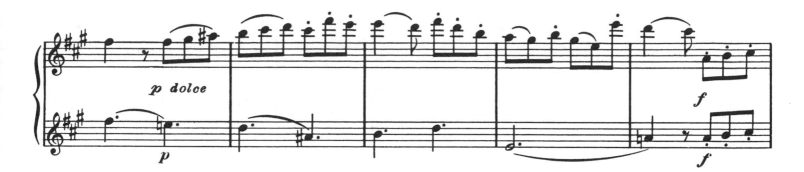

Allegro

9

* After making first D. C. and playing to Fine, segue to last section.

GEMINIANI

10

BERBIGUIER

11

Gigue

BOISMORTIER

12

CAMPAGNOLI

[Allegretto]

13

MOZART

Larghetto [in moderate four]

14

Tambourin

BLAVET

Lively and Lightly

15

Rustic Dance

AUBERT

16

Giga
from Sonata IV

GERARD

17

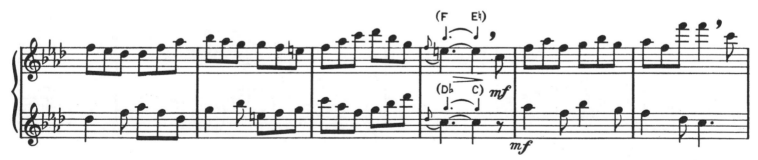

38

GIORDANI

18

19 Allegro

Risoluto

BERBIGUIER

20

TELEMANN

21

Minuet

WEIDEMAN

PLEYEL

Andante

23

24

Maestoso

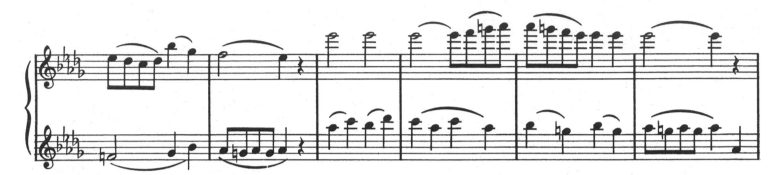

25

DEVIENNE

Allegro

26

Tempo di minuetto

27

Fine

TRIO

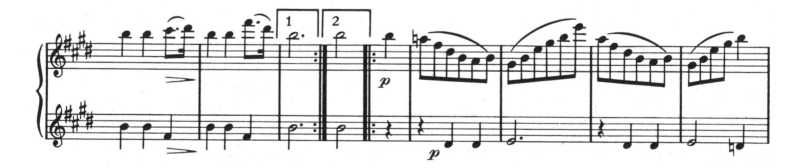

D.C. al Fine

Rigaudon

RAMEAU

Studies in Articulation

The material for this section has been taken for the most part from various standard methods for the flute and the violin.

Play the exercises as quickly as technic permits unless otherwise indicated.

Allegro marcato

23

Allegretto

24

Fine *mf*

ff

D.C. al Fine

25

26

Exercises in Fingering

Practice these exercises slowly and increase in rapidity as the difficulties in fingering are overcome.

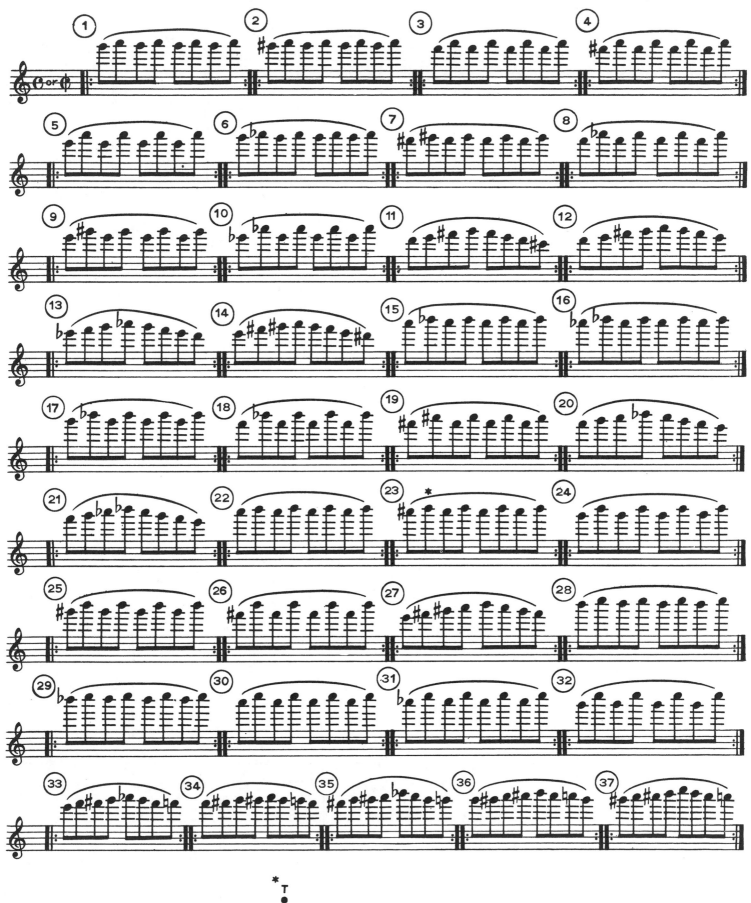

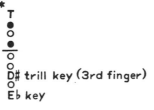

*
T
●
○
○
──
○
D# trill key (3rd finger)
○
Eb key

Table of Trills for the Boehm Flute (Closed G# Key)

Trill with finger pads or keys enclosed by ⁗ ⁗.

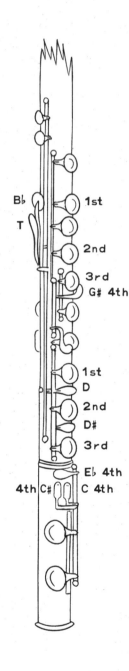

Bb
T
1st

2nd

3rd
G# 4th

1st
D
2nd
D#
3rd
Eb 4th
4th C#   C 4th

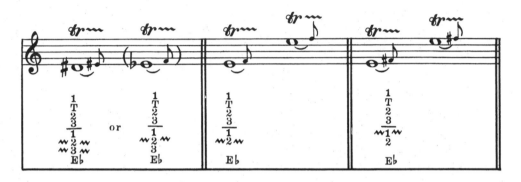

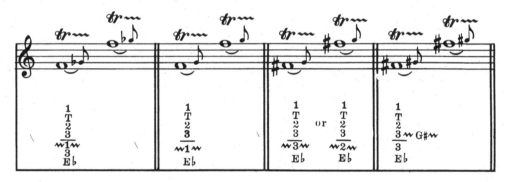

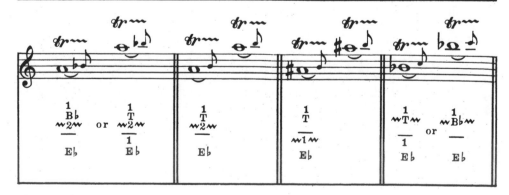

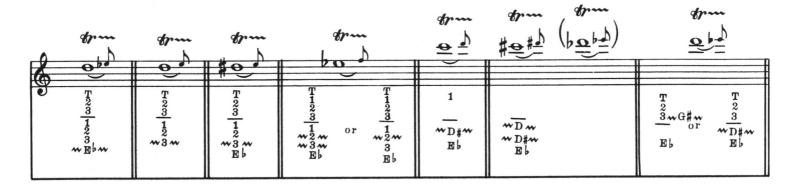

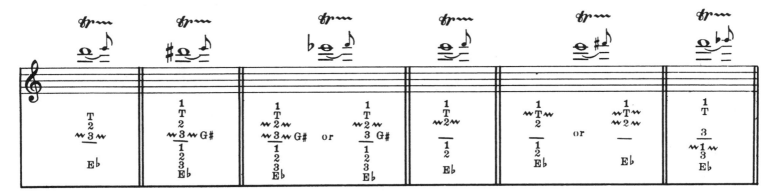

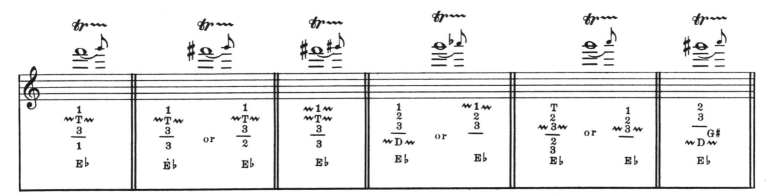

Musical Ornamentation (Embellishments)

In more rapid tempi, trills on eighth notes are frequently played as triplets:

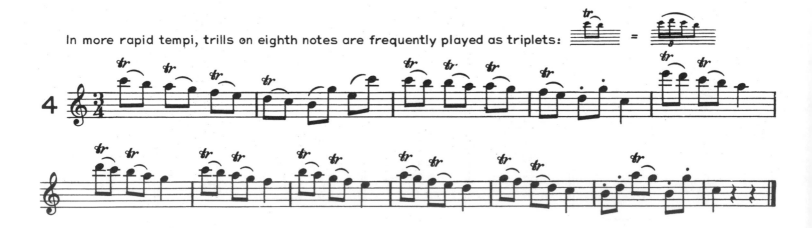

Allegretto

5

To next strain   *Fine*

D. C. al Fine

6

Andantino

PRILL

7

The mordent here is executed:

Long Grace Notes (Appoggiatura)

CAMPAGNOLI

CAMPAGNOLI

* In general, appoggiatura attached to notes divisible by three (♩., ♩., ♪., etc.) receive two-thirds of the value of the main note despite the fact that they may be notated at a smaller arithmetical value. The whole subject of eighteenth century ornamentation is an extremely involved and controversial one. Only some of the simpler problems and their solutions have been included.

The Turn (Gruppetto)

15 Written / Played

16

Slowly

17

Andante

18

Moderato

KLOSÉ

19

DUVERGE

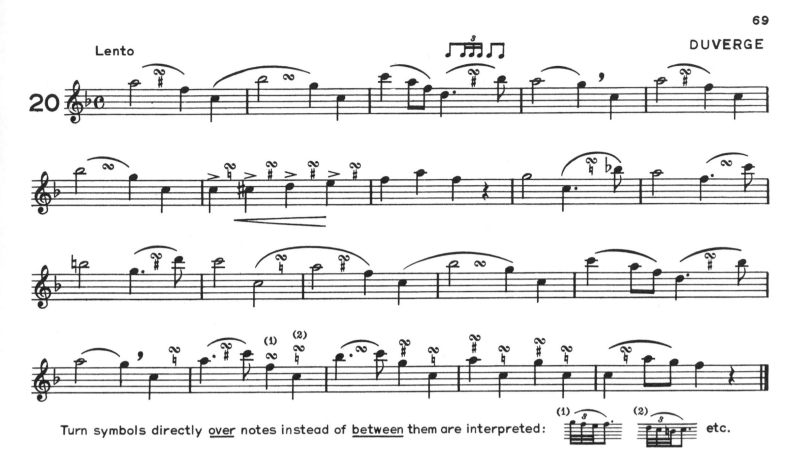

20 Lento

Turn symbols directly _over_ notes instead of _between_ them are interpreted: etc.

In the music of Wagner it is sometimes necessary to play turns that begin on the lower instead of the upper note. The symbol for this turn is ∾.

Excerpt from "Dusk of the Gods"   Excerpt from "Rienzi"*

21

Written
Inverted turn
Played

Regular turn

Inverted turn

* Wagner wrote ∾ but it is traditionally played ∾.

In figures like the trill is generally executed or, sometimes,

22

The music of the time of Bach and Handel (1685 - 1759), frequently contains the figure ♩ or ♩ The time value of the dot is not trilled, the execution being ♩ etc. It should be added that most trills of this period should begin with the upper note.

Sarabande

CORRETTE
(Early 18th Century)

In a stately manner

23

Slowly and sustained

TELEMANN
(1681-1767)

24

Moderato

25

30

31

32

Brillante

33*

34

35

* Flute cadenza from "Capriccio Espagnol" by Rimsky-Korsakoff.

SOLOS

Menuet

from

L'Arlésienne Suite No. 2

BIZET

Largo

from Sonata in B♭

BEETHOVEN

Minuet

DUSSEK

By the Brook

Allegretto grazioso

RENÉ de BOISDEFFRE, Op. 52

Waltz

STEIBELT

Siciliano
from Sonata VI

BACH